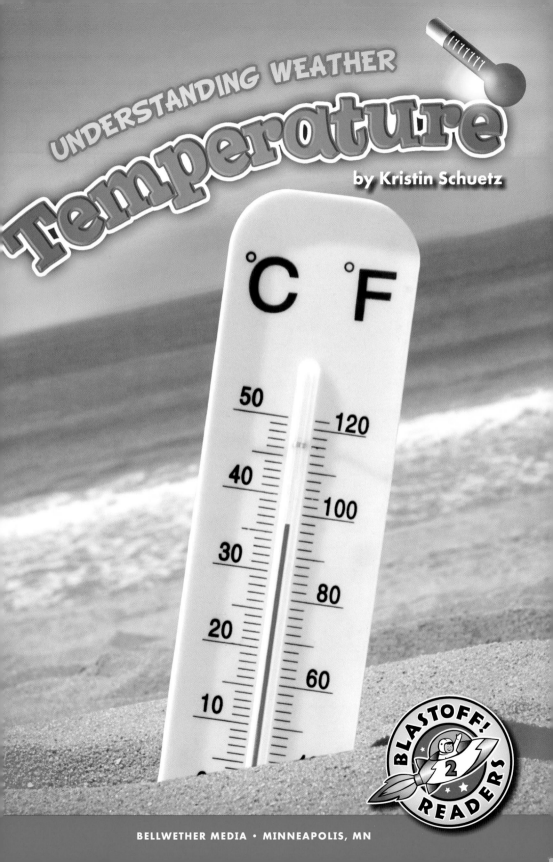

UNDERSTANDING WEATHER

Temperature

by Kristin Schuetz

BELLWETHER MEDIA · MINNEAPOLIS, MN

Note to Librarians, Teachers, and Parents:

Blastoff! Readers are carefully developed by literacy experts and combine standards-based content with developmentally appropriate text.

Level 1 provides the most support through repetition of high-frequency words, light text, predictable sentence patterns, and strong visual support.

Level 2 offers early readers a bit more challenge through varied simple sentences, increased text load, and less repetition of high-frequency words.

Level 3 advances early-fluent readers toward fluency through increased text and concept load, less reliance on visuals, longer sentences, and more literary language.

Level 4 builds reading stamina by providing more text per page, increased use of punctuation, greater variation in sentence patterns, and increasingly challenging vocabulary.

Level 5 encourages children to move from "learning to read" to "reading to learn" by providing even more text, varied writing styles, and less familiar topics.

Whichever book is right for your reader, Blastoff! Readers are the perfect books to build confidence and encourage a love of reading that will last a lifetime!

This edition first published in 2016 by Bellwether Media, Inc.

No part of this publication may be reproduced in whole or in part without written permission of the publisher. For information regarding permission, write to Bellwether Media, Inc., Attention: Permissions Department, 5357 Penn Avenue South, Minneapolis, MN 55419.

Library of Congress Cataloging-in-Publication Data

Schuetz, Kristin, author.
    Temperature / by Kristin Schuetz.
        pages cm – (Blastoff! readers: understanding weather)
    Summary: "Developed by literacy experts for students in kindergarten through grade three, this book introduces temperature to young readers through leveled text and related photos"–Provided by publisher.
    Includes bibliographical references and index.
    Audience: Ages 5-8
    Audience: K to Grade 3.
    ISBN 978-1-62617-255-5 (hardcover : alk. paper)
    1. Temperature–Juvenile literature. I. Title.
    QC271.4.S38 2016
    551.5′25–dc23
                                    2015006564

Printed in the United States of America, North Mankato, MN.

Table of Contents

What Is Temperature?

Some days make you sweat.
Other days make you shiver.

Temperature is the measure of how hot or cold it is outside.

Measuring Temperature

Temperature is measured in degrees **Fahrenheit** or degrees **Celsius**.

FAHRENHEIT vs CELSIUS

Fahrenheit °F		Celsius °C
100°		38°
90°		32°
80°		27°
70°		21°
60°		16°
50°		10°
40°		4°
32°	FREEZING	0°
30°		-1°
20°		-7°
10°		-12°
0°		-18°

thermometer

A **thermometer** is a tool that measures temperature.

A thermometer is a scale. Liquid
inside moves up and down.

The liquid **expands** when it gets hot. The liquid takes up less space when it is cool.

COLD

HOT

Hot Temperatures

Some places can reach 100 degrees Fahrenheit or higher.

HOT! HOT! **HOT!**

THUR

HIGH   LOW

134   62

Death Valley

Death Valley in California is one
of the hottest places on Earth!

HEAT WAVE

MON		TUE		WED		THUR	
HIGH	LOW	HIGH	LOW	HIGH	LOW	HIGH	LOW
60	52	69	60	81	72	95	80

Sometimes extreme heat lasts for days in a row. This is called a **heat wave**.

FRI

LOW
79

SAT

HIGH
81

LOW
73

People must not stay outside for too long. **Heatstroke** can happen.

Cold Temperatures

FREEZING COLD!

MON

HIGH
-32

LOW
-90

In cold **climates**, temperatures often drop below 0 degrees Fahrenheit.

One of the coldest cities is Oymyakon, Russia.

Oymyakon, Russia

MON		TUE		WED		THUR	
HIGH	LOW	HIGH	LOW	HIGH	LOW	HIGH	LOW
60	52	51	42	42	36	29	19

COLD SPELL

A sudden stretch of cold weather is called a **cold spell**.

Wind makes the cold feel even colder. This is called **windchill**.

It is a good idea to stay
inside on freezing days.

The other option is to cover up for the cold. **Frostbite** can hurt bare skin.

Sunday

23 °C
73.4 °F

Min. 11 °C
Min. 51 °F

Humidity
38 %

...dex
...ormal

| ...nday | Tuesday | Wednesday | Thursday | Friday | Saturday | Sunda... |

Meteorologists guess high and low temperatures every day.

Check their **forecasts** to know how to dress for the weather!

Glossary

Celsius—a measure of temperature where water freezes at 0 degrees and boils at 100 degrees

climates—regions with specific weather conditions

cold spell—a sudden period of very cold weather

expands—increases in size

Fahrenheit—a measure of temperature where water freezes at 32 degrees and boils at 212 degrees

forecasts—guesses about what the weather will be like

frostbite—damage to skin that has been exposed to the cold and wind for a long period of time

heat wave—a sudden period of very hot weather

heatstroke—a health problem that can happen if someone is in extreme heat for too long

meteorologists—people who study and predict the weather

thermometer—a tool that measures temperature; liquid moves up and down a scale as the temperature gets hotter or colder.

windchill—how cold the temperature really feels due to the wind

To Learn More

AT THE LIBRARY
Gardner, Robert. *How Hot Is Hot? Science Projects With Temperature.* Berkeley Heights, N.J.: Enslow Elementary, 2015.

Johnson, Robin. *What Is Temperature?* St. Catharines, Ont.: Crabtree Publishing Company, 2013.

Webb, Barbara L. *Hot or Cold?* Vero Beach, Fla.: Rourke Educational Media, 2013.

ON THE WEB
Learning more about temperature is as easy as 1, 2, 3.

1. Go to www.factsurfer.com.

2. Enter "temperature" into the search box.

3. Click the "Surf" button and you will see a list of related web sites.

With factsurfer.com, finding more information is just a click away.

Index

The images in this book are reproduced through the courtesy of: Sergio Stakhnyk, front cover; solarseven,
weather symbols (front cover, all interior pages); majana, p. 4; Chad Johnston/ Corbis, p. 5; Richard Hutchings/
Digitial Ligh/ Newscom, pp. 6-7; age fotostock/ Superstock, p. 8; DenisKot, p. 9; Thierry Guinet, pp. 10-11;
Nas Cretives, p. 12; Amos Chapple/ Getty Images, pp. 14-15; Robert Daly/ OJO Images/ Superstock, p. 17;
Alina Shilzhyavichyute, pp. 18-19; Maridav, p. 21.